Francis William Newman

## The Gospel of Paul of Tarsus

And of his Opponent, James the Just, from our Current New Testament

Francis William Newman

**The Gospel of Paul of Tarsus**
*And of his Opponent, James the Just, from our Current New Testament*

ISBN/EAN: 9783337280994

Printed in Europe, USA, Canada, Australia, Japan

Cover: Foto ©Lupo / pixelio.de

More available books at **www.hansebooks.com**

# THE GOSPEL

OF

# PAUL OF TARSUS,

AND OF HIS OPPONENT,

# JAMES THE JUST,

𝔉rom our 𝔠urrent 𝔑ew 𝔗estament.

---

## BY FRANCIS W. NEWMAN,

EMERITUS PROFESSOR OF UNIVERSITY COLLEGE, LONDON,
ONCE FELLOW OF BALLIOL COLLEGE, OXFORD,
HONORARY FELLOW OF WORCESTER COLLEGE, OXFORD.

---

Neither PAUL nor JAMES ever had a Christian Bible.

———•———

NOTTINGHAM:
STEVENSON, BAILEY AND SMITH, LISTER GATE.
1893.

# THE GOSPEL OF PAUL OF TARSUS AND OF HIS OPPONENT JAMES THE JUST.

PAUL OF TARSUS is our earliest authority in Christian literature. Among his popularly received Epistles one alone is certainly not his, and does not bear his name, the Epistle to the Hebrews. To class it as Paul's, is mere wilfulness. Of the rest, which bear Paul's name, no adequate reason leads the present writer to reject any: and four, viz.: (one to the Romans, two to the Corinthians and one to the Galatians) are received as *authentic* and *genuine* by the most scrupulous critics. His public life as an ardent Pharisee began (as estimated by our divines) two years after the crucifixion of Jesus, and closed (as church tradition teaches) by the Emperor Nero's executioner, A.D. 64, six years before the Roman Destruction of Jerusalem. No esteemed Christian antiquaries can place our earliest gospels, Mark and Matthew, so early as A.D. 80. Hence all Paul's Epistles carry a date earlier than our earliest received Gospel. This simple fact was open to all students from really primitive times. Its immense importance is not yet seen by more than a very few English Protestants. That is why it seemed to the writer an adequate reason for pointing to Paul as our source of History.

## PAUL THE PHARISEE.

Paul began his public life as a zealot for the law known by the name of Moses, and was driven into the persecution of the Christian deacon Stephen, not by personal bigotry, but by the express command of the law. But the causes of this "first martyrdom" are widely mistaken; a fact which calls for the opening of details.

The moral and spiritual superiority of Israel to all known empires, hardly excepting Persia, depended on the strict upholding of the Divine Unity. Their God is called in Deuteronomy THE ONE LORD. Towards any one who teaches a second Lord, no pity is allowed; the rulers and the populace are commanded to stone him, though he be, to any of them, son of his mother. This is the sole offence for which the law enacts the penalty of stoning. Unquestionably in Acts vii. the penalty of Stephen's offence is stoning. Evidently the High Priest and his assessors and Paul himself believed that in their action they were simply obeying *the law*. Therefore they held Stephen's offence to be other than that alledged in the Acts; in their interpretation he was teaching the people to honor *a new god whom their fathers had not known.* That the account given in the Acts is incomplete, is in several ways clear.

First of all, it is distinctly stated that the legal action was taken, *not at all against the Apostles.* They were in no complicity with Stephen. In chapters iii., iv., v., the Apostles plainly announced the coming back of Jesus into glorious rule, which implied the superseding of existing authorities; and it gave no offence. If Stephen now *was not supported* by the Apostles, and they were not suspected of aiding him, he must have started some new doctrine of his own. And the narrative proceeds to tell us, that Paul was commissioned to persecute the sect of Stephen, if he found any of them in Damascus, and (as Paul himself says in Acts xxvi. 11), " I persecuted them even to strange cities." Now, even if it be true that at this time, some partizans of Stephen were slain *in* Jerusalem itself, while the Apostles were untouched, the narrative is, not defective only, but deceptive. Stephen must have headed a schism in Jerusalem by preaching *a new creed* which the Apostles refused to sanction and must have drawn off converts to his own doctrine, yet the narrator represents Stephen as "full of faith and " power," without a hint that he was leader of a new sect, which the Apostles disowned. The Stephen who has been called the *proto-martyr* is then also the earliest heretic, who when elected to distribute doles of food to the poor, busies himself chiefly in embroiling the Apostles in religious faction and bringing needless danger on disciples of the new Messiah.

Certainly the narrative cannot have had the sanction of the Apostles, when it paints Stephen as angelic in aspect, and correct in faith, while teaching a doctrine which they did not approve. What then really did he teach?

The speech of Stephen in his own defence is given at much length in the Acts, yet it explains nothing, it denies nothing, and does not enter the argument *of the law* at all, but evades the matter in charge. Fair time is allowed, and silent attention, until he seems to show that *he has no defence*, except to turn against his tribunal by violent attack. Thus he convinces them of his guilt in bringing into honor a new god Jesus, of which therefore evidently no Apostle had been accused. A rush is made against him and the penal process of stoning is called for. He exclaims that he sees Jesus standing at the right hand of God, and dies with the Invocation of Jesus on his lips. Jewish Elders well knew that among the Gentiles the Invocation of a dead man was the earliest and easiest beginning of Idolatry. With Stephen it cannot have been the first time, and as such they resented it, in strict conformity to their law.

This first dreadful stage in the life of Paul of Tarsus makes him for ever after a mysterious man. He had sacrificed his tender nature to the demand of a law esteemed by himself and his nation as the sacred command of our Supreme Disposer; but after awhile, (we know not how soon) all seemed to him inhuman and horrible. He pitied his victims, eminently Stephen. He adopted the faith, not so much of the Apostles, as more nearly of Stephen himself, and to us it seems inevitable *that he must condemn the law,* which positively enjoined the death of Stephen by public stoning. But so uncalculable is the mind of this man, that he continues to call the Law *holy, just and good,* while treating its commands as made only for the unrighteous, for children and for slaves, commands which to all righteous men are superseded by their higher spirituality, and in his last Epistle he commends the Hebrew books as divinely inspired.

The conversion of Paul from a Pharisee to a Christian is the most important fact in Christian History next to the Crucifixion of Jesus. In the Acts his conversion is several times narrated as effected by a great miracle visible in the sky. Paul lay under his Roman graveyard more than forty years before the book of Acts was written, and when Paul (himself writing) tells of his own conversion (Gal. i. 16) he speaks only of an internal change within himself, in which no second person could see any miracle; yet not only was the fact wonderful, but the permanent state of mind was in many ways so strange as is hard to comment on.

## Paul the professed Christian Apostle.

To us Paul's primary value is, as a contemporary witness of Christian facts : for without his guidance as a living man, vast uncertainty would remain, where through him we now see clearly.

As a first specimen we may observe that the cool, and one may say the bitter, attack of Paul on Peter in Galat. ii., especially with Peter's later meek, sweet and unpretending First Epistle, (which I suppose to be genuine), convicts at once as falsity the whole idea of any supremacy lodged in Peter by Jesus. If there were a particle of truth in it, it must have been in the beginning notorious to all the Apostles and to every new convert. Paul could not have been ignorant of it. Yet Paul behaves as if the plain duty of Peter, not to add of James and John, were to listen to Paul's wisdom and accept Paul's gospel revealed to him singly.

To us this is very important, for it at once sweeps away as invention later than the life of Paul, all idea of supremacy granted by Jesus to Peter, and fundamentally overthrows Romish pretensions from the time (say) of Hildebrand.

A second equally important fact is the doctrine of Paul concerning Jesus as taught in 1 Cor. viii. 5, 6, "Though (to the Heathen) there are gods many and lords "many, yet unto us there is but *One God*, the *Father,* "(*out of* whom are all things) and *one Lord*, Jesus Christ, "*by* whom are all things." Paul is so accurate in contrasting Christ, as God's *agent* in this world, with the Father who is the *source* of all, as to leave to Athanasius no pretence that the Father and Christ are the same in *essence*. Elsewhere, as to the Colossians, Paul avows that the Heavenly Christ was the first born of all creation, and the same phrase is adopted by the Apostle John in the Apocalypse (iii. 14) who calls Christ *the beginning of the creation of God*, showing that both set forth GOD and the LAMB as two entities, and that the Eternal was the creator of the Lamb. Thus Paul, the Apostle of the Gentiles, held an essentially different doctrine from Athanasius, as did also Arius hold, as the doctrine of the Gentile Church, transmitted from Paul, its originator. But as Athanasius so deviated from Paul as to make the Creed unintelligible; Paul so deviated from the earliest teachers as to make his Creed essentially diverse. It cannot be pretended that Paul merely stript Judaism of its ceremonies; for his addition to the primitive creed was at once a vital destruction and a vast transformation. The details must here be named.

It has been seen, by the account of Acts (viii. 1.) that the Apostles were in no complicity with the offence of Stephen, who was convicted of bringing in *a second god* by Invocation of the dead Jesus. All learned teachers knew that this was the first step into polytheism. Now in nearly every Epistle Paul shows the same proclivity to invoke Jesus as an Omnipresent Spirit of unknown and indefinite power; that is, *a second god*. We have no proof that during Paul's life any of the Apostles concurred with him. But Paul went beyond anything reported of Stephen: for he maintains to the Philippians that Jesus of Nazareth *had lived in a heavenly form* before his human birth; and elsewhere, as in 1 Corinthians viii. and to the Colossians, that this same Jesus was the earliest born of divine creation, and acted for God as his substitute in creating. The very idea was probably new to every other Apostle and to nearly every Jew that had not like Apollos imbibed Pauline or Egyptian teaching. It seemed to mean only that Creation was a task too tedious for the One God. Paul's new creed was meant to be the Power of God and the Wisdom of God, learned by him (such appears his argument) when caught up into Paradise; but to all other mortals it was only through Paul, by Paul's own Wisdom. Elder Christians did not universally unlearn Jesus to learn from Paul. Jews had hitherto understood from their Law, their Prophets and their Psalmists, that to penitent sinners, confessing their sins, God's arms of love were open, *without any sacrifice*. Sacrifice was not appointed for THE GUILTY. For moral guilt, as for common theft, or disobedience to a parent, or for a grave sin like adultery, no sacrifice was imagined. The real objects of sacrifice were twofold, *first*, as matter of cleanliness, if one have unawares touched a corpse, or anything defiling, or if a woman have given birth, or a priest have made an error; NEXT, (though this reason was not needlessly protruded) because the family of the priest or Levite *fed on the sacrifices*. In no case *did* or *could* any sacrifice relieve one tainted by moral guilt. For such sin, in estimate of Jew or Christian, the sole process was, *Repentance of heart, Confession,* and (if the case required it) *Restitution* to any one injured, and NOTHING MORE, if the crime did not require *death.* God's mercy sufficed for even scarlet sin. To the really penitent, sacrifice was superfluous; while for him whose guilt required the forfeit of life, *all doctors of the law* held that DEATH ABOLISHED CRIME. Even when the Pharisees had adopted from the East the doctrine of the Resurrection of the Just, no belief taught the resurrection of the wicked. (It is not here alledged that the doctrine of an Eternal Hell was ever Paul's doctrine. On the contrary, in his Epistle to Timothy (1st Ep. ii. 4) and even iv. 10, he says: " God is the Saviour of all men, *especially* "*of those that believe.*" Paul nowhere implies Eternal Punishment.)

Undeniably Paul has fastened on the Gentile Church the Homeric idea that blood shed by a butcher is an acceptable sacrifice to God — (see Galat. iii. 13, also Ephes. v. 2), " an offering for sacrifice of sweet savour." Alas! he has made the thought to Englishmen who are called Evangelical more than prominent. It is not rare to value the doctrine of Christ's Deity as *useful* chiefly for validating the blood-power. " Without a *God* to bathe you and himself in his own blood, how can you get forgiveness of sin?" is addressed to us as serious argument. It is thought quite self-righteous to believe the whole Old Testament until it is corrected by Paul's doctrine that the sacrifice of the first created angel by a Roman executioner was previously counted on by the Father of Mercies and God of all Comfort as a sweet-smelling savour. As I write, I wonder at myself for whom well-nigh forty years of life were needed to disenchant me of Paul's glorious and captivating eloquence.

As we have no scrap of defence from the men whom Paul assails, we cannot with confidence accept his coloring. For it is clear that Paul had no means of knowing Jesus himself, and no tenderness for the older creed which he thought it his business to destroy.

Christian Jews remembered brothers and sisters of Jesus, and their parents, Joseph and Mary. The idea that Jesus had, or could have, any *higher* title than PRINCE (of Israel) and Saviour (from Gentile oppressors) was no part of the original creed. The new doctrine of Paul, that Jesus before his earthly birth had been a Heavenly Spirit, may not always have shocked disciples in Jerusalem; at most it may have been pondered reverently. But Paul's sole argument for that novelty, and all his monstrous novelties, is given by him to the Corinthians, that he learned them in the third heaven, when he was caught up into Paradise; (whether *in* the body or *out* of the body, he did not know!) To gain any attention to such a tale, at least needed some corroboration; but he offered none.

Yet with Paul this was only a beginning of change. The most precious of possessions to every true Jew, and not the less for his devotion to Jesus, was the book of the magnificent prophet who celebrated their return from Babylon under the patronage of the Great Cyrus. It fills the pages in our Bibles under the false heading of "Isaiah," after the fortieth chapter. The prophet deals with Israel as distinct from Gentiles, promising to Israel in the future a glory *double of all his shame* in the past. Jesus, while alive, had strictly enjoined obedience 'to the rulers and the Mosaic law. All before Paul had obeyed him. Paul now had the hardihood to reverse the prophet's plain words, and strip them of their special interest to Israel. Paul, by his own sole authority, obliterates from the tablets of the future every possible consolation that they held out to the Jew, however carefully the prophet may have guarded Jehovah's promise.

We do not know, even approximately, the dates at which the apostles learned Paul's distressing eccentricities. The mere words in 2 Cor. xi. 2–6 are more than enough ; but the very frank reminder of his earlier warnings to the Galatians given to them by Paul himself, proves to us that he had entirely *expected* resolute opposition of *his gospel* to come from influential quarters where *another* gospel would be preached, so different from his, that he even refuses to call it another—(Galat. i. 6–9). With a solemnity equal to an oath, he reminds them of his first declaration to them, "If even an angel from heaven "preach to you any gospel different from mine, let him be "accursed!" At what wicked heads is he striking? It was not convenient for him to say too plainly, and we moderns have written as if to propagate historical truth were bad policy. To disown this thought is to the present writer needless.

We have to consider contrary facts, though only a few can here be presented to the reader. Yet we may at once say, that the Apostles collectively in the first stage, and James the Just in every stage, were opposed to Paul, and James always preached a gospel which Paul despised.

*(A)* James preached the old fashioned gospel which he had imbibed from the lips of Jesus. He had learned from childhood that Circumcision was to all the seed of Abraham an everlasting covenant, and accepted by Jesus himself. James dared not reject it, nor encourage any to throw off Moses in putting on Christ.

*(a)* Paul does the very thing which James disapproves.

*(B)* James and the Apostles who had known the living Jesus, were well aware that Nazareth at large, and the disciples, had always received Jesus as a human prophet, however exalted. No talk of Jesus as an Angel before his human birth, had place in the Gospel of Jerusalem. The Apostles mourned over the cross and knew no reason to thank God for its wickedness.

*(b)* Paul gloried in the cross as the sole means for the forgiveness of human sin. Luther could find no symptom of this in "the Epistle of Straw," *i.e.* of James.

Unlearned English Bible Readers, such as I was myself at the age of thirty-five [though not unlearned in Latin, Greek, Arabic and something beside], will probably assume that Christians of Jerusalem under James believed in Jesus as certainly higher than human, though they may not have known how much higher, and *must have* believed in his Atonement for Sins, as Paul did. At present I say merely that Paul in his charge *by word of mouth* to the Galatians, "*to curse* any one who preached "to them a different gospel than his," was by anticipation warding off a mild remonstrance from James.

When Christians from James came to persuade Galatians to accept, not the *Christian* hope only, but with it the *Jewish* political glories, Paul could no longer contain himself, and with his own hand he wrote to them the Epistle which urged them *to curse* those, whose doctrine (he said) *made Christ to have died in vain.* (ch. ii. 21.)

Here was the crisis of difference. Before Paul, the principle had not been admitted that the cruel death of Jesus was in any way to be *rejoiced* in. Paul inferred, "Then Jesus died in vain." Paul saw it as overthrowing the Law of Moses, a first advantage,—and as forgiving human sin, a second. On neither side did the elder Church see with him. And to these Paul's curse was alike fierce and unbearable. We may all now read James's meek but firm remonstrances. (James iii. 5–18.) Concerning Faith and Works, James cannot reply so directly. He may not quite understand Paul ; but on the one hand, he judges every worshipper by *Deeds*, not by *Profession;* next, he does not account Mosaism slavery, rather to a true born Jew the law of Liberty ; lastly, he does not with Paul talk of Faith in *Christ*, but only of Faith in *God*, in addressing his kindred the Twelve Tribes, whom, while faithful to God, he cannot disown as inheritors of the Israelite Kingdom. He was likely to prefer a reasonable and modest Jew to a browbeating Christian.

But we are treading here on Paul's weakest side, and it would be more pleasant to celebrate his excellent foresight in superseding much that could not stand. Among other matters it is notable that nowhere in his many and ample Epistles does he allude to Jesus as having in his human life *ever wrought a single miracle.* Nor can we make light of this as a negative fact to which it did not suit him to allude. When miracles are so prominent in our four Gospels, they must have been notorious (if they

were true) not only to every disciple, but to every
Galilean, nor could the total absence of miracles have
been the standard reproach of hostile Jews against the
arguments of Christians. [Yet this is Paul's distinct
utterance], that God, wishing the weak to conquer the
wisdom of the strong, refused to give to the Jews the SIGN
that they required (*i.e.*, some miracle), a remark which cuts
two ways: first it denotes that Christians at Jerusalem
had no habit of trumpeting great miracles wrought by
the living Jesus; next, however grandly Paul himself
talks of *his own* "demonstrations of the Spirit and of
"Power" (1 Cor. ii. 4), he does not mean anything which
either unconverted Jews or now any Protestant Arch-
bishop would accept in modern phrase as a *miracle*. In
Paul's lifetime not one of our four Gospels was current.
He could not mean to contradict them. Yet I claim to
make a first digression now, to show that the Gospel of
Matthew is no sacred book, but only an ignorant Legend.


### DIGRESSION ON LEGEND CALLED MATTHEW.

No esteemed critics place its composition and publication
in present form earlier than the Destruction of the
Temple by Titus Vespasian.

In the opening Pedigree the two names Ahaziah and
Uzziah are confounded into Ozias, and the two inter-
mediate names Jehoash and Amaziah are dropt, thereby
losing three generations. Also another generation is lost
by confounding *Jeconiah* with his father Jehoakim, whose
name is omitted. This discovery first showed me (more
than fifty years ago), that *I must unlearn my power of*

*counting* if I continued to believe that a petty mistake or blunder was "the work of the Holy Spirit." King James's translators *cannot have dared* to notice it.

Wilder and grosser is the miraculous birth of Jesus, *without any human father*, suggested by an ignorance of Hebrew, which neither Paul nor King James's translators could commit. For they must have read in Joel (i. 8)

> "Lament, like a VIRGIN girded with sackcloth for the HUSBAND of her youth,"—

words which even to one ignorant of Hebrew show, that the English translation has manufactured a false miracle. But that is not the whole stupidity involved. For the promised child was a pledge from Jehovah to King Ahaz PERSONALLY, who died many centuries before the birth of Jesus. In the second chapter we are informed that King Herod slew all the children under the age of two years, near Bethlehem, *in hope of killing Jesus*. Now we have the history of this king from Josephus, the Jewish historian, who details his atrocities without scruple, but makes no allusion to this slaughter of infants. Matthew tells us that wiseacres taught Herod that the new Christ was to be born (according to prophet Micah) in Bethlehem. But Micah's Christ was to triumph when the Assyrians came into the land. But the Assyrian power and its very site had ceased to exist five or six centuries before the birth of Jesus. This writer cannot have been anything but an ignorant Gentile.

In Matt. ii. 15, a quotation (as from a Hebrew prophet) is made of Jehovah's words "Out of Egypt have I called "my son," words perversely applied as though in order to bring Jesus *out of* Egypt, God sent him *into* Egypt. Rather it seems the writer was bent to find such a text,

and readily snaps at the words of Hosea concerning
*ancient Israel* with no possible reference to Jesus.
Presently he makes it said *of Jesus* "by *the Prophets*," He
shall be called a Nazarene; but no such text is found.
These two chapters are remarkable as treating dreams as .
of *divine authority*. So much is here enough. But when
Jesus has appointed twelve Apostles, he sends them with
authority to the twelve tribes, and with power, saying
(Matt. x. 7): "Heal the Sick, Cleanse the Lepers, Raise
"the Dead, Cast out Devils! *Freely ye have received, freely
"give.*" The words are unlimited. They are either a
magnificent fact, or a magnificent fraud, which, for more
than 1800 years, have deceived not merely babes and
sucklings but full-aged and wise men, whoever received
"Matthew" as a *sacred* book, and eminently in this nine-
teenth century our Anglican Church and our Bible Society.
And if these words were true, how could any Apostle
be ignorant of the fact, and how could Paul ever have
encountered from well-informed Jews the complaint that
Jesus and his Apostles had given no valid *sign?* But we
need not appeal from Matthew to Paul. It suffices to
listen to Matthew himself. In ch. xiii. 54 — 58, after
Jesus comes into his own country and has refused any
*sign* (vii. 39) [calling those who mildly asked for what
(we are told) he had so liberally announced, an EVIL AND
ADULTEROUS generation], Matthew tells us that Jesus did
not do many mighty works among those who remembered
his brothers and sisters, and his two parents Joseph and
Mary, because of their *unbelief!* Surely, the writer
should have thought of this, before he made Jesus say:
"*Freely ye have received,* freely give," if in those of
his own country unbelief was a sore impediment to Jesus

B

himself. Moreover in ch. xvii. 19–21, what to men of those days seemed the easiest of miracles, *the casting out of a devil*, proved too hard for his disciples: thereupon Jesus is made to explain to them that it is because of *unbelief* in the Apostles themselves, and this *kind* of devil needs prayer and fasting: so that " Freely ye have received" is a mistake, and there was no free gift to them at all.

I beg now to take my reader back to Matt. iv. 23–25, and see the vast profusion of miracles there narrated on multitudes of the sick from distant places, without a single difficulty, and to Matt. xi., when John the Baptist sends to ask whether Jesus is the expected Messiah, and the triumphant reply of Jesus as a successful miracle-worker. When the same narrator presently confesses that in Jesus's own neighbourhood he found unbelief so prevalent that he did few " mighty works," does not this suffice to stamp as foolish credulity of a later age, all the glibly flowing tale of miracles which no one who saw them has narrated ? I think every one who demands reasonable evidence for a miracle, must see that Matthew and Mark, who tell us that Jesus walked upon the water, no more deserve our attention than when they or others attribute to him the going about *"doing good,"* when all that they tell *credibly* is, that with twelve (or if we prefer, seventy) mendicants, he aided to eat up the households of the poor, instead of Paul's very different method.

Passing to the two last verses of our Matthew, we find two matters to remark on, a command of Jesus to baptize the Gentiles, and that, in the name of the Holy Trinity, moreover a command to teach all his precepts to them. Yet when Cornelius and his party are baptized, in Acts x., the Church at Jerusalem is offended with Peter for admitting Gentiles, and Peter when thus called to account, does not defend himself by the obvious topic : "This is "the very thing that the Lord Jesus in his parting words "commanded us to do," although *ten* other Apostles were at hand to corroborate him; but instead of falling back on the command of Jesus, behaves as if he had quite forgotten it, and defends himself by a new vision or dream. Are we to imagine that of the eleven Apostles *all* had *forgotten* the parting solemn words of their Master? I reply for all men of good sense: "They had "*not* forgotten, but Jesus never gave them such command. "It was invented *for* him by the fancy of these compilers, "Matthew and Co.," and this solution accounts for the fact, that the eleven Apostles between the death of Jesus and of Paul *never thought of teaching to their converts the precepts of Jesus*, nor of baptizing in the name of the Trinity, nor, until Peter's dream, had they learned to admit Gentiles to baptism. The objection of the Church showed no particle of bigotry; but on hearing of Peter's dream, they glorified God (xi. 18) with joy.

Clearly then, whatever we read within the covers of Matthew, is so far from being commended by these covers, that however natural and reasonable it may seem, it remains only possibly true, and in no sense has the *prima facie* aspect of *historical truth*. When men expect us to believe in miracles on ANONYMOUS REPORT, they expect folly from us.

In comparison to the anonymous authors of these Legends, Paul is a sensible man, yet his claim to be listened to is such as no modern (unless Swedenborg be excepted) would gravely propound. In 2 Cor. xii. 2–4, he indirectly declares that either in the body or out of the body (he knows not which) he was caught up into the third heaven and heard in Paradise words unutterable. A man in these days would be thought a fool or a madman for such fancies. Even if he in many respects were wise and lofty in character as Paul, it would be utterly unreasonable to claim belief for his power of distinguishing Divine Visions from Human Dreams. Still, Paul never pretended to work miracles, much less that a person *unknown to him* had worked them *unseen by him*. Such philosophy lies in another plane from Paul, who at most barely *hints* at the *possibility* of a miracle from him. It is pleasanter to listen to his wisdom and to be struck by his fervor than to criticize him.

Still, his claim to know who was *the earliest creature of the Supreme God*, carries with it overwhelming self-refutation. If I had learned from him this mystery and were asked for my source of knowledge, I could only reply: "Ask Paul; he speaks the wisdom of "God in a mystery." Nay, but surely a trance or a vision may as easily be "the folly of man," and carries no guarantee of being the "wisdom of God."

Next, if Christ is above Paul, the Apostles whom the living Christ selected are higher than Paul, who does not pretend to have been appointed by the living Jesus, but only by a Jesus of whom we know nothing. No Apostle of Jesus *can* have believed this tale. How did it ever gain currency? The explanation is easy. Of all Christians Paul was necessarily the most persecuted. He had given intense provocation, he earned attack most righteously, and had endured it bravely and unshrinkingly. This made him a Power, and of this Power he shows himself amply conscious. His last words to the

Galatians express it. "Henceforth let no man trouble me, *for* I bear in my body the marks of the Lord Jesus." He knew what weight a well-battered form added to a preacher's opinion. The eleven must early have known it, and respected him, while they differed from him and feared him. They must have early understood that he went far beyond the limit of Stephen, from whom they had dissented, but to accept his doctrine about the Cross as atonement for human sin, was too much. That he still called the Law which commanded the death of Stephen *holy, just and good,* while he trampled it under foot, was among his riddles.

James fought an honest battle for his Master's old creed, with no ambition of raising novelties or claiming for Jesus *any loftier place than he had himself claimed.* But to Paul, and, we may believe, to Pauline converts, especially to Gentiles, the creed of James may have seemed not honorific enough for a Messiah who was to *come back from death* and become Divine Judge of Jews and Gentiles. Hence when the Church of Jerusalem disappeared with the city, and both Paul and James were slain, the creed of Paul superseded the creed of Jerusalem, *until Athanasius displaced Paul.*

Meanwhile Paul gives us new instruction, when he enforces the *Resurrection* of Jesus, in 1 Cor. xv. We now learn that the Pharisees did not understand by it new life of the *flesh,* but solely the carriage of the *soul* to heaven. We might expect the same from Paul, who though he renounced the ceremonies, yet prided himself as a genuine Pharisee. He distinctly calls Resurrection of the Flesh a folly, and attributes to Jesus after death only a glorified form, such as no one, if called to witness, could recognize by memory of the living Jesus. Here also Peter aids us, if the Epistle which bears Peter's name shows Peter's doctrine ; for it distinctly says: "Christ was put to death *in flesh*, but made alive *in spirit.*" This is earlier than our Gospels, earlier than A.D. 68.

This fifteenth chapter is in several senses *unworthy of Paul*, but further to criticize his weakness is hardly needful. All will feel this, when courage to criticize is earned, though one may not understand being baptized in behalf of the dead. By falling back on this wonderful topic and appealing to us by a question, which seems to mean, "What is the use of it?" he unawares reveals how little his heart's trust rests on the risen Jesus as seen by 500 disciples at once. But now for the first time I become bold enough to expound my view of Paul in Galat. ii. (which attacks Peter with Paul's own friend Barnabas) side by side with 1 Cor. x. 20—22, "Unto "the Jews I became a Jew, that I might gain the Jews ; "to them that are under the law as under the law, that "I might gain them that are under the law : To them "that are without law, as without law, being not without "law to God, but under the law to Christ, that I might "save them that are without law. To the weak I became "as weak, that I might gain the weak : I am made all "things to all men, that I might by all means save some." Clearly this is the very "DISSIMULATION, " which in Galat. ii. 13, he so sharply charges on Peter and on Paul's own coadjutor. How is Paul to be reconciled to himself ? This for half a century I could not explain. A simple thought at length strikes me, and with it I become suddenly bold and reveal it to my reader, "*either* Paul had not yet written "1 Corinth. (so says the margin of my Bible), *else* he "forgot what he there wrote," and inasmuch as Barnabas, his avowed coadjutor, took Peter's side against Paul at Antioch, the true solution is that at Antioch Paul was wrong as *to the facts*, for neither Peter nor the "Judaizers" tried to *compel* any Gentiles to be circumcised; that was merely Paul's *perverse misinterpretation;* but even James forbade (ecclesiastical) *compulsion*, and neither Peter nor Barnabas was so favorable as James to Jewish ceremonies, but only went so far as to claim for every Jew a right to *persuade* any Gentile convert in guise of a Jewish Christian (Isaiah lxi. 5-6) to be a High Minister of God, rather than "as a Gentile and son of the alien" to be a Ploughman or Vine-pruner to saintly Jews. The idea of such a humiliation for Gentile converts was to Paul so agonizing, that he could not, on the one hand, fairly interpret the prophet; nor on the other, allow to James, Peter, or even to Barnabas the right of interpreting to the Gentiles the Hebrew text. This solution leaves Paul in possession of *his own* claim to be all things to all men; i.e., what to us means HIS RIGHT TO DISSIMULATION, a right (or wrong) which he refuses to other Jews *who do not claim it*, though Paul is too hot-headed to understand them.

Nothing can be clearer, than that *if* any Christian Teachers laid on Gentile converts Circumcision as *necessary to salvation* (Acts ch. xv.), they had no support from the leaders in Jerusalem. But since Pharisees who made proselytes to Judaism seldom went to this length of bigotry, it seems more probable that the phrase *necessary to salvation* is the mere error of an ardent Paulist who wrote fifty years after the events.

Another matter is to be considered. We know from Paul

to the Galatians, that earlier after his conversion, perhaps three or four years, Paul went to Jerusalem and abode with Peter fifteen days. (He adds, we hardly know why, a solemn oath, that of the other Apostles he saw none but James.) Nevertheless fifteen days with Peter were long enough, *if Peter were aware* that he had seen Jesus walk on the Lake of Tiberias, and *even* once feed thousands of human beings in the desert with a few loaves and five small fishes, which left a surplus of twelve baskets full — then I say, all modern Christians will confess that Peter had plenty of conviction to impart to Paul how marvellous a miracle-worker Jesus had been: moreover, how apt a pupil in sacred miracle was Paul we learn from Paul himself, who, without even a Hebrew text, convinces himself, that when the rod of Moses had opened a spring in the desert, the rock itself (spring and all?) *followed* the people's march, and (he adds) "this rock was Christ." Here was a listener with ears wide enough open for Matt. xxvii. 51—53, if Peter had been able to guarantee them, and how much more the two great miracles of the 4th Gospel? But it occurs to me, that if Peter could have produced from that 4th Gospel the tale of " Incredulous " Thomas " (John xx. 26—29), Paul's reply would have been quite different; for his "risen Jesus" had no deep wound in his side in which Thomas could lay his hand. For absurd materialism like this, Paul had *no taste*. We see this even in the Holy Tongues, as treated by him, in 1 Cor. xiv. He is ashamed of them; for he says, "An "unbeliever, coming into a Christian congregation amid "such chatter, will think them *mad*." Paul seems to have put an end to the "Holy Tongues," by insisting that unless accompanied by *an inspired interpreter*, they were inexpedient. Yet he dared not simply discard them, but even said, "*I thank my God* that I speak with tongues "*more than ye all*," words which seem to run to the edge of "vanity."

While Paul's ignorance of any miracle wrought by Jesus nearly disproves all such miracles in our Gospels, it must not be forgotten that no such miracle is alledged by any known writer within fifty or more years after the death of Jesus, and this in itself is sufficient reason for refusing belief.

Paul, trained under Rabbi Gamaliel, might naturally have been an accomplished interpreter of his nation's sacred books. He does not approve himself to European scholars now as such, whether in his simpler or in his controversial Epistles. The "Acts" several times celebrate the power by which he proved that Jesus was the Christ; but not once in all his writings does he seem aware that before he can take up this problem, a previous question must be solved, viz.: Whether prophets who anticipate the kingdom of God, all speak of it as introduced by one and the same Messiah; whereas their obvious sense is that under King Hezekiah, though Isaiah's root of Jesse (in Isaiah ix. 6, 7 and xi.) seems even greater than Jesus of Nazareth, yet the history shows in fact no such great king for either prophet, and each assigns his task to destroy the power of Assyria. Also the Son of David prophesied in Psalm lxxii. cannot be found, and the like remark applies to other Psalms and to David, and in none of his Epistles does Paul quote from Hebrew prophecy what marks any intelligent forebodings of the real life of Jesus. But in Paul we first find the corrupt use of Prophecy (or imagined Prophecy) to give us information of *hitherto unknown* history. One example here suffices, because with great simplicity Paul reveals his mental process and complacency in it.— Romans xv. 2—4 :

> "Let every one please his neighbour unto his good for edification.
>
> "For, even Christ pleased not himself."

After this Paul reveals to us, *how he knew the fact. Not* from those intimate with Jesus during his life ; *but,* from a verse in the sixty-ninth Psalm, which *Paul judges* to speak of Jesus :

> "But as it is written, 'The reproaches of them that reproached thee fell upon me.'
>
> "For whatsoever was written aforetime was written for our learning, that we through patience and comfort of the writings might have hope."

How great a weapon this doctrine afforded for writers of sacred history, we may see in the Epistle called 2 Peter i. 18, "We have also *a more sure word* of pro-"phecy (more sure than words from Peter?) to which "ye do well to take heed, &c."

As Paul *inferred* that "Jesus pleased not himself," because Paul read a certain verse in Psalm lxix.; so possibly Matthew after Paul's death wrote xxvii. 35, because he found the words in Psalm xxii. 18, and supposed it was written with foresight of Jesus; so too from Psalm lxix. 21 the tale of Matt. xxvii. 34.

In our fourth Gospel even a peculiarity in the death of Jesus is deduced from a Mosaic law concerning the Paschal Lamb, "a bone of him shall not be broken." Instead of asking what facts already known as history may be justly looked on as fulfilling a prophecy, the

*Rabbinical logic* assumed by Paul rather lays down as the problem, What unknown details may be claimed as History, if thereby comfort and hope may ensue.

### EFFECT OF PAUL'S THEORY OF THE CROSS.

THE power of Paul's doctrine on the human heart cannot be denied. James, like his Master Jesus, could only preach to sinners Repentance and Conversion,—an old story, very necessary, but very unpleasing; bitter in the mouth, if sweet in digestion; while Paul says, " God " himself entreats you by me his messenger to be " reconciled to him, enemy by nature as you are. He " has sent from heaven *his own Son,* who was a mighty " angel in heaven, highest of created beings, who at " God's bidding, took human flesh, endured human " miseries, and paid the ransom of your souls : accept His " offer, give yourself to Him, the only true God, and for " the sake of His Only Son, your Redeemer, live in grati- " tude the life worthy of one who is redeemed by such a " price."—Once at least Paul adds, " Know ye not that ye " shall judge angels ? " To so lofty an eminence does he lift feeble mortals ! God chooses the offscouring of the world and babes in knowledge to confound the wisdom of the wise.

James had no such net as this to catch human fishes for his gospel. Paul's subtlety to entice Pagans and avoid Paganism is truly remarkable. It has been ob- served in the History of Christianity that its Corrupters have based all their meanest doctrines on texts attributed to Jesus ; but its Reformers have generally found their strength in the doctrines of Paul. In England and its offshoots we see the tendency in our two extreme schools to be either ritualist or Pauline. Paul must have heard the Attic Legend of Prometheus, who from love to mankind wilfully incurred the anger of Jupiter our enemy, and was (we may nearly say) crucified for it in Mount Caucasus. But if the tale ever dwelt on Paul's mind, he ingeniously *de*-paganized it. To us his "father of "heaven" was no enemy, as in the Greek fable, but was the Father of Mercies and God of all Comfort; and our Redeemer was no rebel against God, but the dutiful First-born of all creation, a Son on his Father's mission to suffer cruelties for our benefit and as an example to us; cruelties which the One God could not undergo, because He is unchangeable and too great and cannot suffer.*

Paul knew this attribute of the Eternal Father, and never confounded him with Jesus, while for the Father himself he always retains the purely Hebrew ideas of Holiness and Love. These seem unknown to Pagans, whether we look to Æschylus, Socrates and Plato, or to Cicero, Seneca and Epictetus. Thus Paul did his best against the bad side of his own creed, and perhaps in his Arianism bequeathed the best truth which Gentiles could then receive, though against this the death warrant of Stephen had been signed. But when the Paulinists had so exalted Jesus, that disciples could exist who made Godhead unintelligible (not merely incomprehensible), all good sense vanished, indeed had no room possible; and

---

* The writer of the Epistle to the Hebrews, evidently of the school of Paul, is strongly on the side that Christ *must suffer:* therefore it seems hardly credible that our text (Hebrews xiii. 8) can be sound, which claims for Jesus *eternal unchangeableness.*— To me the words " Jesus Christ " appear the after-garbling of an Athanasian.

free fancy painted up the mother of Jesus into a still more amiable being than Jesus himself. Then out of saint-worship inevitable Polytheism budded, yielding Asia to Mohammed, who gathered degenerate Christians into a rivalry of which to this day we see no beginning of the end; but Paul, by his first step of corrupting Jewish Monotheism, may be thought virtual author of the sequel.

He claimed for his gospel the motto for every convert: "Thou art bought with a rich price, the blood of the "Son of God." It runs through his Epistles, and is cardinal with our English Evangelicals. In the poor and simplehearted, who speak freely, it often comes out, that the object of their TRUST (and thereby of their love) is the Son rather than the Father. "I have told my sorrows "to my Jesus: I was sure he never would forget me," is a phrase that fits the lips of many "a babe and suckling." I repeat it as I have known it, not to attack Paul, but to suggest how easy is our remedy, which, if Paul could now arise from the dead, after 1800 years, without any return of Jesus from the clouds, Paul himself would be likely to adopt,—viz., we must revert to old Judaism, and pass back *to the One God* all the fire of devotion which Paul has kindled for the glory of his "first-born "of all creation." Not that Jesus "died in vain;" but simply, God never *approved* his cruel death, nor smelt it "as a sweet savour." (Ephes. v. 2)

## RETROSPECT OF LIFE OF JESUS.

No portion of the short life of Jesus was so likely to be reported to us accurately by local tradition as its first fatal Passover, when Jews from abroad were assembled at Jerusalem. Whether well or ill affected towards Jesus, his summons before Pilate moved intense interest. Every part of the trial had been public, and Pilate, anxious to give warning to future insurgents, carefully wrote above his cross—

THIS IS JESUS, KING OF THE JEWS.

Roman practice demanded, especially under the strict and scrupulous rule of the able Tiberius, clear explanation of local severities. If Pilate could have elicited from Jesus any intelligible disavowal of his claim of royalty; if he had been able to assure Tiberius that Jesus, like a Stoic philosopher, counted himself a king and all human kings to be slaves, but had no thought of subverting the Roman rule, and looked solely to angels from the clouds to set up his kingdom, we know that Tiberius would have only smiled. When pressed to punish a man for impiety, he replied: "If the gods are "wronged, the gods will look after the culprit." But a governor whose negligence shed Roman soldiers' blood in local broils, was sure of disgrace under Tiberius. Matthew tells us that Jesus had hoped for twelve legions of angels to help him against Pilate. Whether this is strictly true, we do not know; but something of this hope may have stiffened the resolve which Paul (2nd Ep. to Timothy) praises, to persist in asserting to Pilate his royalty. Yet despite of his miserable death, no vengeance from Heaven has followed in this lapse of eighteen centuries.

It is the habit of all these Legends, as of Romances and of Fairy tales, to speak with innocent confidence, however wondrous the tale, without a hint how the writer knew the story, much less asserting that he was an eye-witness.

In the Legend called Luke, on which we next speak, is a small but possibly notable difference of conduct in the *robbers* whom Pilate crucified on both sides of Jesus, as if implicated in his guilt. Pilate having no animus against Jesus, can hardly have volunteered a gratuitous insult; and in Luke the two robbers are made to say to Jesus, "If thou be Messiah save THYSELF and US," most natural claim of men who had taken arms in the name of King Jesus. On trying this possibility, we at once find it probable as well as possible. For it will account, *first*, for the robbers' petition to Jesus, as natural; *secondly*, it makes Pilate's acquittal of Jesus impossible; *thirdly*, it makes Jesus's half-and-half behaviour, which previously seemed as if he were courting crucifixion, the only conduct we could expect from him. With his consciousness that his recent preaching on the side of Jordan had allured these brave men into insurgency, he knew that no disavowal of intended revolt could alter the doom due to himself or them, and he preferred to stiffen their patriotism by the utterance "It is not for a *fancy* that you lay "down your lives, but in the cause of your *own legitimate* "*king*." Hence to disavow his kingship formally was like a new disgrace.

But besides these three arguments, a prefect like Pilate knew how to please *the just and anxious Tiberius*, if after dispersing a troop of men who had raised the standard of King Jesus before it swelled into numbers which might capture an arsenal, Pilate could announce, "By the "sacrifice of only three fanatical lives, and without the loss "of a single Roman, I have crushed the first beginning "of an obstinate religious war." The writer of such a message knew what praise it would earn.

On the whole therefore, and until a better explanation is suggested, I believe that the two "robbers" were insurgents who bore the flag of "Jesus Son of David."

If Jesus was conscious that his own royal tramp through Jericho to Jerusalem had roused these new followers into real insurgency without his intention, *then*, on finding that Pilate's vigilant cavalry (?) had anticipated his slow movement and arrested two of his partizans, he knew that any disavowal of intended royalty was vain and ignominious, and left him as the only decorous action to persist in a simple claim of just royalty.

By this theory we acquit him of a voluntary resolution to perish, when frank truth would have saved him. If he knew that these two "robbers" had been arrested for proclaiming his royalty, he knew that in no case would Pilate dare to acquit him. Each acted under constraint after his plunge, of which he well had known the danger.

The Legend current as Luke's is edited by an unknown writer in better Greek, who honestly tells us, not that he has divine command and aid, but that he has tried to follow the tale from its earliest; also, it is as the churches have been *catechized*, a phrase which suggests the second century.

His *pedigree* of Jesus follows a line different from Matthew; yet each clings to *Joseph* whom neither allows to be the real father of Jesus. Also this Joseph was in Luke the son of Heli, in Matthew son of Jacob. Trifles here warn us of graver error.

The celebrated discourse "on the Mount" in Matthew, and "on the Plain" in Luke, has more important contrasts. In Matthew we read: Blessed are the poor in spirit; but in Luke, Blessed are ye poor, also Woe unto you rich; for, ye *have received* your reward. What of these very discordant utterances? The contrast suggests the terrible parable of Dives and Lazarus, and the question whether that parable is really from Jesus, is one which I am reluctant to touch. The rich man is in hell, not because his riches were ill-gotten, but because he had had his consolation on *this* earth, and there ought to be a *balance* in the other world. This seems false and pernicious doctrine, but it is made the heartless reply of Father Abraham to the rich man's piteous entreaty. He assures him that the gulf between heaven and hell is *impassable*, as though God, instead of a Being of ever-enduring mercy, were a stern and unrelenting tyrant.

Unhappily the same bitter tone, opposite to good, of an undying worm and unquenchable flame, pervades so many discourses attributed to Jesus, that they have leavened, or rather poisoned, all Christianity, although they are not Pauline, and barely Apocalyptic (as applied to real persons, but only to *abstractions* such as the Beast and the False Prophet). Contrary to Paul's Father of Mercies and the Psalmist's God whose mercies endure for ever, the God of Jesus is one to be *feared* as casting soul and body into Hell! This hideous picture, the worst side of Christianity, appears to have colored all Mohammedism, and established Coward Fear instead of Reverent Awe as the basis of religion.

Besides, we find in Luke the disgraceful parable of the steward who cleverly cheated his master, held up for imitation with the suggestion, "So make yourselves friends by "the mammon of *unrighteousness* (his phrase as a stigma

c

on wealth) " that when ye fail *they* may receive you into
" everlasting habitations." Surely this is a false version of
Jesus ! Yet it is current as sacred and divine ! I respect
both Jesus and his chief Apostles too much easily to
believe Luke correct.

Nor is it worthy of a prophet from heaven, when a
rich man asks what he shall do to inherit eternal life, to
reply, "One thing thou lackest, sell thy goods, distribute
" them to the poor, *and follow me.*" The exhortations of
Paul of Tarsus are surely better and wiser.

But unhappily we have no account reasonably trustworthy, as to the REAL precepts of Jesus. These Legends
were written too late in time, in a foreign tongue and
by persons evidently incompetent, moreover false miracles
blight their trustworthiness.

FOURTH GOSPEL, CURRENT AS " JOHN'S."

THE three preceding narratives were written by men
ignorant of the demands of *truthful* history and of its
*difficulty;* by men credulous and blundering, yet not
consciously false. But to careful modern inquirers it is
certain that this fourth writer had no intention to
write *what we call* truth of history, but merely a
brilliant romance, profitable to the soul to believe, if
it could.

Concisely as the case admits, the argument will be
here stated. First, as to the time when this Romance
came out. Nearly every book in our English Canon
belongs to one of two classes—(1) The coming back of
Jesus from the clouds of heaven is earnestly and speedily

expected. To this belong the three first Gospels, the Acts, all the Epistles of Paul (except that to Philemon), the Epistle to the Hebrews, Epistle of James, 1st Epistle of Peter, and the Apocalypse. (2) *To the latter* belong the three Epistles of John the Presbyter of Ephesus, the fourth Gospel, the 2nd of Peter (so-called), and the Epistle of Jude. Time needed to pass before it was possible for the Church to resign the hopes which had raised them out of despair into the confident hope that Jesus would return with angels out of the clouds of heaven. The many retained the fond hope after the ablest men (as St. Jerome) rejected it with the Millennium as a Jewish fable, though it was cardinal with Paul and in the Apocalypse. But whenever it vanishes from the Canon, the date must be later in time than the other class.

Nearly our earliest Church "Father" is Justin the Martyr, who wrote a Defence of Christianity to the Antonines. Their reign is from about A.D. 160 to 180. He may have been slain about A.D. 172. He knew nothing of four Gospels, yet seems sometimes to quote from one or other, by the title *Records of the Apostles.* The fourth Gospel is generally in the style of the Epistles of *John the Elder* (Presbyter of Ephesus), who *may be* the author; but there is no proof that John the son of Zebedee was the writer, and the suggestion is scarcely possible by chronology.

The date A.D. 180 is the earliest at which we can prove the fourth Gospel to have been known as such, i.e., 116 years after the death of Paul, who, in Acts vii. 58, is called a young man. Evidently any *new* facts concerning Jesus are not mere *romances*, but *frauds*, to which I hope no reader of these pages will give a gentle name. The romancer's object is clear by his omitting all the devil-miracles (prominent in the other Gospels, but ridiculed by educated heathens), while retaining the grand miracle of feeding thousands in the desert with obviously insufficient food; but shifting the scene from the lake and desert to Jerusalem, he invents two miracles *wrought under the hostile criticism of the rulers*, and publishes them thus late in time, after Jerusalem and its priests had vanished. By the two miracles are meant, the giving sight to a man after forty years of pure blindness, and restoring life to Lazarus after he had been four days in the grave. Obviously such miracles would have been trumpeted to every open ear, and notorious to every disciple. When no previous Gospel mentioned them, the omission suffices to prove them false. The whole narrative is visibly a slander on the common Jews as well as on the rulers,—a slander still more base than that of the three first Gospels.

Jesus, even in this Gospel (v. 44), speaks of God as known to the Jews as *the only true God*, and in xvii. 3 says in magnificent prayer, " This is life eternal, to know " Thee *the only genuine God*, and Jesus Christ whom Thou " hast sent."

Some words of a late Anglican, Rev. Frederick Denison Maurice, may here deserve to be quoted : ·

" I hold, cheating with words is in all respects more wicked, as " well as more mischievous than cheating with cards. The man who " does the latter act is playing with a worthless instrument; he pro- " bably injures men who are as great rogues as himself, or dupes " who may be saved from future ruin by present loss. He brings " into discredit that which one wishes to be discreditable ; the

" other is blasting thè holiest and divinest implement; he is
" making the whole commerce of life suspicious ; he is leading
" the most earnest men into despair of it, damning the only object
" which is worth living for.  If the one is banished from the
" fellowship of his own class, ought not the other to be excom-
" municated by all good men ? "

Such words from F. D. Maurice are not only very true,
very brave, but also very necessary in the opinion of the
present writer, to whose indignation against the fraudu-
lent fourth Gospel, the following reply was made in the
*Modern Review*, an English *(Unitarian)* organ, of July,
1881, by one specially chosen to refute me.  The following
are his words :

" All difficulties of the fourth Gospel fall away at once, when
" we note, that this Gospel is not and *does not intend to be* a source
" of information concerning *the historical Jesus*, but is a profession
" and testimony *of faith*, put forward a century after his death."

The italics here are mine.  We have only (he tells us) to
*note* that *the false writer does not intend* to be a source of information concerning the historical Jesus, when he boldly
tells *as historic fact*, that the Word was *made flesh* and John
the Baptist *saw* him and *testified* to him when he (the
Word) dwelt among us, and *we beheld* his glory, full of
grace and truth.  *Truth* is in this Gospel a very prominent
word, and now a learned man tells me that all difficulties
vanish, if *I will note* that *he does not intend* to tell historical truth, when he professes to tell it !  No ! he only
makes profession of FAITH !  So Faith is not even a
profession of Truth !  To me this seems to say, that as
soon as *I note* that in his solemn pretence of loving
truth he merely loves and practises lies, all difficulties
vanish.

As yet I have only known Unitarians as lovers of Truth, and as believing that the God of Truth cannot bless a lie; therefore every lying spirit is in Unitarian judgment hostile to God. But now to my surprize I find in a Unitarian organ, a man to whom, on the gravest topics, false history is no offence.

Surely unless this Gospel is honest error, its great cleverness or beauty only makes it more hateful. I do not understand how any one who regards it as historically false, can preserve neutrality towards it, much less read texts of instruction from it without any necessity, in a nation devoted to the Canon supposed to be Divine.

Another matter must not be omitted. Matthew tells us (xxviii. 16, 17) that the eleven disciples went into a mountain of Galilee to see Jesus after his crucifixion, and has the honesty to add, "But some doubted." Here was a grand opportunity for the ingenuity of a writer a century later, and he cleverly seizes it. Forgetting Paul's phrase *Thou fool* to one who believed in Resurrection of the Flesh, or making sure that no Christian would call him to account, he takes "Thomas" as his specimen of a doubter, who wants to put his fingers into the prints of the nails in Jesus' hands and thrust his hand into the spear wound [words which are thus made to confirm the New Gospel] or he will not believe. This gives occasion to the risen Jesus for a majestic speech to Thomas, and eliciting the reply, "My Lord and *my God!*"

Apparently the magnificent speech imagined for Jesus in ch. xv., xvi., xvii., was intended to supersede the miserable utterance of My God, why hast thou forsaken me? (if indeed that is not a mere adopting Psalm xxii.

for History). But we are constantly in these Legends forced to doubt how much is historical.

James and Paul had no written document as a reconciling creed, yet their common conviction that Christ would *soon* come back enabled them to delay any quarrel till he should sit in his tribunal. His return was vehemently predicted in the three Gospels, and though we cannot at all infer that James had heard it from his Master, few will doubt that with Peter and John he partook in the sentiment which pervaded the early Church after its first Pentecost, and Paul's First Epistle to the Thessalonians exhibits *his* version of this same "by the "word of the Lord." Yet after 1800 years nothing of this has been fulfilled.

Time makes us wiser than Paul. If Mohammed had predicted his *speedy* return in the clouds, we should regard such lapse of time to confute him of false prophecy. I now need only say, Mohammedans will justly use the plea against Christianity, for the Christian Church itself has practically for more than 1500 years ceased to believe in the Earthly rule of Jesus returning as he went up.

Again and again it may have occurred to my reader to ask, How is it that when by our New Testament (as we read it in its authorized text) so much is clear, yet National Protestantism *has never aimed* to attain a Creed older than the fourth century, and still clings to formulas unknown to Paul and James alike?

The causes are really on the surface of History; but hitherto the knowledge of History has never pervaded a nation, and neither students nor philosophers exist in mass. Public Policy seldom can aim at Truth; and without large Political aid, the more Reform is needed the harder is its achievement. Luther and Calvin would have alienated a vast mass of Protestants, if they had deviated too widely from the creed of Rome. By the excesses which followed the change of a single ceremony (that of the *Baptists*), Luther was so terrified, that Conservatism seems to have really predominated in all his thoughts. Not to alienate princes, was as necessary to him as to our Cranmer. Except in the short reign of our Edward VI., seekers after Truth had scarcely a free hearing. The new Creed made a fixture of Bishops endowed with power to *absolve or retain Sin*. Our great Queen Elizabeth dreaded Rome in politics only, but desired puppets in her preachers. Under the Stuarts free thought issued in defiance of the State, and then found mere self-defence a task more than enough against a hostile Church and State.

But the last sixty years open to the world of Protestants new events and new thoughts. Samuel Taylor Coleridge first expounded to us that a Church Establishment had its true function in National Education, and Arnold, of Rugby, entitled the tithes and other funds as happily saved from the scramble of selfishness. Ecclesiastical funds, more and more, are felt to be, because National, wrongfully made Sectarian or Private; and the recent history of the Protestant Church in Ireland now warns us against either alienating the funds to private hands or yielding them to a Sectarian Convocation. We more and more mourn over our Sectarianism, and discern that only by retaining in impartial hands as Trustees absolute right to the property can we thwart unjust waste of Public Funds.

It is not much, to say that our Clergy no longer lie in the same slush as under our Four Georges. Two new names enter our High Church; they are Broad Church or Ritualist. Concerning the latter, nothing is here dropt; but the former include a mass of learned men, who understand History and will neither neglect nor pervert it. Happily a beginning has been made to *permit* them to publish Truth in Historic Research. Their task is, to teach the zealous but reluctant Evangelicals, and the first thing needed is to raise them above the slavery of unchristian creeds. Then under the light of Christian History they will convert nascent *piety* into *wisdom;* Britain will forget Sectarianism and will worship the One Holy Glorious God in a single Church, more wisely than was possible for our ancestors, however pious their purpose. Our Established Church must make its Creed rightfully honorable to the wiser men of all nations: then she will absorb her own sectaries without a struggle.

The fact must be very disagreeable to every Christian (as it was to me some fifty years ago), to discover that in no extant writing have we trustworthy detail of the *words* and *deeds* of Jesus. I am now comforted, on finding that it is the all but universal case; possibly therefore no calamity. Buddhists, Parsees, Hindoos, Mussulmans, Jews, are *in one boat* with Christians. Neither Paul nor James had a Christian New Testament: neither of them seem even to have been conscious of a loss. The Jews did not know what *we* know—that the Pentateuch (as a whole) was not so old as King Josiah. One thing very important we know, that the Precepts called CHRISTIAN have approved themselves to blessed saints for near two millenniums, and while we have our living God and

D

Christianity, we shall not miss Jesus, though he never come back in a choir of angels. God does not allow Wisdom and Truth to perish with the life of any mortal prophet. The inward history is never recoverable.

Christianity *without Christ* is the best religion that man can now get; for it means—

All that is best in Judæo-Christian religion,
Without doubtful genealogies or doubtful mythology,
Without Saint-worship or False Gods,
Without Rabbinical fancies or Oriental incarnations,
Without the Eternal Hell or the hideous idea of Satan,
With the fixed certainty of the Human Will, capable
    of Sin or Holiness,
With the One Lord of heaven who has no lord,
Who is essentially good and wise; and from us men
    demands
Love of Mercy and Justice, with humble Reverence
    to God.

What more can man wish, but more Goodness in man, with much more GOOD SENSE than hitherto?

Paul, with obvious errors, is a noble moralist and a fervent votary. To avoid his weakness, and attain his virtues, is a worthy life-struggle.